Angels
The Divine Connection

Elisabeth Stein, Ph.D.

EST - P.O. Box 4363
Tallahassee, Florida 32315-4363
© 2003

For information contact
Elisabeth Stein, Ph.D.
P.O. Box 4363
Tallahassee, FL 32315-4363
Angels-TheDivineConnection.com
850.386.5978

Dedication

To my two very special angels

who comfort and inspire me

Erika and Monika

Table of Contents

Acknowledgements

This book would not have come into being without the help of the angels and the support of my wonderful daughters, Erika Elisabeth Frisby-Moore and Monika Jeane Johanna Frisby. The encouragement and moral support of my daughters and my friends, Ursula Morgan, Susan E. Tucker, and John D. Simons enabled me to keep working even during times of considerable stress. I greatly appreciate their generosity for the time they dedicated to proof reading and offering many helpful suggestions. In addition, invaluable contributions in editing were made by Erika Elisabeth Frisby-Moore. I am also grateful for the inspiration and support I received from Mark Victor Hansen and Robert G. Allen.

Angels to the Rescue

It was a dark moment in my life. Alone and at the edge of sanity, reeling with emotional anguish, screaming to God for help, I begged Him to relieve me from the excruciating agony. Writhing in pain I rolled into a fetal position. Suddenly a warm cloud enveloped me, and I sensed a presence that I could neither see nor explain. I felt embraced, cradled, surrounded by love. The heaving in my chest eased, my eyes were no longer flooding, and an inner peace washed over me wiping away the pain that I had felt just moments earlier. I fell asleep with the comfort of a baby being cradled.

That ranks among the most powerful angel experiences of my life. It was more powerful than the experience of seeing angels in my bedroom, and more powerful than the time when the bus ran over me but didn't because the angels intervened and stopped time.

My fascination with angels began one day when I was vacationing at Cedar Key on the West Coast of Florida. I wanted some alone time and chose this remote island for its pristine beauty and lack of commercialism. The room I checked into was on the bottom floor of a three-story condominium. That night I had a horribly realistic nightmare about a man crawling through the window of my room about to rob me when I woke up in a cold sweat. I was so terrified that I went to the registration desk and asked to change to a third-floor room. After bringing my luggage up three flights of stairs, I immediately felt comfortable in my new room. I headed for the balcony, when I suddenly felt a tap on my shoulder. I turned around and saw no one, but I was aware of a presence. I went into the bedroom and the presence was definitely with me. I asked "Are you from God?" and immediately felt a comforting warmth. So I stayed.

What does it mean when we are visited by angels? I am convinced angels are not just visitors but that we each have a guardian angel who stays with us at all times. There is no other way to explain the phenomenal experiences I've had throughout my life.

Every visible thing in the world is put in the charge of an Angel.
— **St. Augustine**

Angels of the Past

As a perpetual student and college professor, research is second nature to me. Thus, it was only natural to study angels. The word "angel" comes from the Greek and means messenger. Nearly all major cultures on earth have winged figures in ancient art. The first winged beings date back to the Etruscan era before the Roman Republic nearly three thousand years ago. The Greeks introduced the winged goddess of war and the goddess of victory. Of the two, the Nike remains famous today, although the wings are now more commonly seen on running shoes rather than a beautifully clad goddess.

Angels seem to make their appearance in art at critical turning points in history. They appear in legend and literature two thousand years ago during the birth of Christ. St. Thomas Aquinas writes about them extensively during the height of the Dark Ages and the violent Crusades. Paintings of angels

Nike of Samothrace
The Greek Goddess of Victory

become particularly numerous during the Renaissance and the Baroque Period, a time when the schism of the Catholic Church divided its adherents into two volatile camps, the Catholics and the Protestants. Once relative peace was established at the end of the seventeenth century, angels

withdrew from canvases and sculptures.
They began reappearing again toward the
end of the twentieth century amidst fears of
the end of the world, Y2K, and the recent
increase in terrorist activities.

In the early 1990s, angel books occupied
one or two shelves of major bookstores.
Angel pins, jewelry, and angel figurines
were found only occasionally in gift shops.
Today, angels in a variety of artistic forms
can be found anywhere gifts are sold. They
are back! Why? Most probably because of
the uncertainty of the times.

Ours is the age of terrorism and
uncertainty. If there is one thing angels are
good at, it is protection during times of
turbulence. After all, these are the angels
that stood by God when the legendary
Lucifer convinced a third of the heavenly
beings to challenge God's authority in
heaven. Lucifer and his cohorts lost the

battle and were cast out of heaven. Where are they now? They are the negative energy that permeates weakness and doubt. Where are the good angels? They are around us protecting us from the dark angels, and from the weakness to which we might succumb.

The biggest obstacle the angels have to fight on our behalf is fear. Fear of being alone, fear of being hurt, fear of losing our possessions and our health, and fear of losing loved ones can paralyze us. Angels pierce the veil of fear and rescue us from our own weaknesses, when we let them. Angels cannot interfere in our lives without our permission. So when we ask, they are there to help.

I asked when I realized the school bus driver didn't see me. I thought it was the end. Almost instinctively I called out "Angels, please help me!" There is no logical or physical explanation for what happened.

It was during a heavy downpour. I was driving in the right-hand lane. The school bus was next to me and changed lanes, moving directly into me. Although it seemed impossible, time stopped. I was alive, and the school bus was in front of me. I can't explain it, but I know it was real.

Do I understand angels? No. That's why I have been studying them for twenty years. When I began giving angel lectures and angel seminars, I was amazed at the number of people who responded with genuine interest and personal angel experiences. They can be found in all walks of life, from the homeless person to officials high in government positions. At the angelic level, we are all the same.

An Angel can illumine the thought and mind of man by strengthening the power of vision, and by bringing within his reach some truth which the Angel himself contemplates. — St. Thomas Aquinas

Teachings of the Angels

So what did the angels teach me? Oh... where do I begin? Fear was my biggest stumbling block. Beginning with fear of the dark and fear of being laughed at in childhood, to fear of death and fear of failure as an adult, I can honestly say today that thanks to the angels, I am no longer afraid. For me that is a quantum leap equivalent in size from the flea to the elephant. I love my two daughters more than life itself; I no longer live with constant fear for their safety. An inner knowing keeps me calm. It's taken five decades to get here, and it was worth every step. It is the angels who walked this path with me. There were many times I forgot about their existence, but they never forgot about mine.

I can't tell you how I know; I just know that each of us is blessed with a guardian angel. Our guardian angel is available to us at all times through the power of thought. That is the secret.

The secret is that we create our lives and our emotional well being with our thoughts. It is the wisdom of the ages from the beginning of consciousness.

Biblical wisdom for three thousand years has maintained that "as [a man] thinketh in his heart, so is he." (Proverbs 23:7). The Roman Emperor Marcus Aurelius wrote "You become what your thoughts make of you." Four hundred years ago Shakespeare proclaimed "There is nothing either good or bad, but thinking makes it so." And in the twentieth century, Earl Nightingale's *The Strangest Secret* proclaims that "You become what you think about all day long." The famous psychotherapist who coined the concept of the Collective Unconscious, Carl Gustav Jung, observed that "Your own vision will become clear only when you can look into your own heart. Who looks outside, dreams; Who looks inside, awakes."

To some extent we are all dreamers. From childhood on we dream of our present and our future. Some of us may even have talked with imaginary friends in childhood. These invisible friends were probably angels we were able to see until our visions and dreams were educated out of us by well-meaning parents and teachers.

When life challenges us with crises and painful loss, parental and academic teachings rarely serve us in dealing with anguish and grief. It is in our most vulnerable moments that the angels are closest to us. Even when we don't ask for help, angels are there. How sad that we are not taught to ask. Only churches remind us on occasion that Jesus suggests: "Ask, and it will be given you; seek, and you will find; knock, and it will be opened to you. For every one who asks receives, and he who seeks finds, and to him who knocks it will be opened" (Matthew 7:7-8).

Sometimes we do ask, but we tend to get discouraged when we think our questions or requests are being ignored. We are never ignored by the Divine. The problem is that when we ask, we have something very specific in mind. If our request is not met with exactly what we expected, we often don't notice that we did get an answer, but of a different kind than what we expected. I like the saying, "Sometimes God answers our request for silver by giving us gold." It is unfortunate when we can't see the gold because we are looking for the silver.

When I prayed for a teaching position and didn't get it, I was deeply disappointed. I had just graduated from college, and at the time there were more teachers than jobs. I had dreamed of being a teacher since first grade. All I wanted was my own classroom, but the only job I could find was working full time in a typing pool. I applied to every school within a hundred-mile radius of where I lived, but there were no openings, no silver and no gold. Then I found out I would be able to teach as a teaching assistant if I went to graduate school. So I applied and got my classroom and eventually my Ph.D. I got the gold, but it took quite a few years! Had my initial prayers been answered, I would probably still be in one of the elementary, middle, or high schools to which I had applied. I would be happy because I love to teach, but evidently God and the angels had other plans for me. Becoming a college professor was a dream I hadn't even dared to dream when I sent out all those applications years earlier.

So the secret of life is to focus on positive thoughts, to ask for help, not only from God and the angels, but also from family and friends. Sometimes even strangers are willing to help. The following five-step process has worked for me:

5 Steps to Your Dreams

1. See your dreams and desires clearly. Write down what you see in your mind's eye. Be very specific. Put a time frame on your dreams. Pick a date on which your dreams are to become reality.

2. Express gratitude for the reality of the dreams in the NOW (present), and believe with all your heart that it is yours.

3. Think positive and creative thoughts of how you can turn your dreams into reality. Dismiss negative or discouraging thoughts which interfere.

4. Ask for help from others, human and divine. Build a dream team with like-minded friends. Don't confide in anyone who might rain on your parade.

5. Act. Work to bring about what it is you want.

Doubt and Fear

Following the five-step process seems pretty simple. If it is truly that easy, why aren't we all living our dreams? There are several reasons why creating what we truly want and getting angelic assistance in the process seems to be relatively rare. The two biggest obstacles are doubt and fear.

Although I have a very deep faith and truly believe in angels, doubt occasionally blocks my vision. It is not the angels' existence that I doubt, but my own ability to clearly discern their messages. On a number of occasions, I've gotten a feeling, but didn't know what to do with it. For example, I was asked to present a seminar and just didn't feel like preparing for it. This is very unlike me. I had been working intensely on another project and had gotten very little sleep. I just couldn't force myself to stay awake to prepare the seminar and got very angry with myself for not getting the work done. Several days before the scheduled presentation, I received a phone call that the seminar was cancelled. Instead of looking at the cancellation as a lost opportunity, I breathed a sigh of relief realizing that my body had listened to angelic guidance and I had gotten the badly needed sleep. When I made the connection, I realized I had not gotten the angels' message because I was tormented by the fear of not being prepared for an important presentation.

He will give his angels charge of you, to guard you in all your ways. On their hands they will bear you up, lest you dash your foot against a stone.

Psalm 91:10-11

The Dark Angels

Fear and doubt are shadows that hide inspiration and thwart creativity. They are the dark side that challenges the light. They are the fallen angels that keep us from seeing, hearing, and feeling the divine messengers of God.

The view that everything in this world is only good and that no evil exists is unrealistic and dangerous in a universe that operates on opposites. Where there is light, there is also darkness; where there is cold, there is also warmth. So logically, where there are good angels, there are also bad angels.

The Bible calls the bad angels the fallen ones because they fell toward earth after being thrown out of Heaven following their revolt against God. Since God is Good, the fallen angels are seen as fighting the Good. Since they were cast out of heaven, it seems logical to assume that their battle against the Good continues in the world.

Unfortunately, it seems our fears cause us to pay more attention to the efforts of the angels of darkness than to the angels of light. This interest is reflected in the news media's focus on crime and violence. Maybe we just want to know what's out there so we can be prepared. But exposure to so much negativity makes it difficult for us to keep our own focus on the positive.

How can we tell when in our daily lives we are influenced by a fallen angel?   An easy way to determine whether a voice, a vision, or a thought is coming from the dark or the light angels is the feeling we have during and after our experience. Fear and doubt are not always what they seem to be, but what is unmistakable is the feeling they produce. Sometimes it's just a mild discomfort, and sometimes it shakes our very foundation.

Several years ago, I had an offer from a small private university in California for an administrative position that paid much more than my salary as a college professor. Because the offer included teaching, I considered it, visited the campus, and met several of the administrators. While the campus was beautiful and most of the people I met were very cordial, I had feelings I didn't understand. Something inside me felt uncomfortable, but I didn't know why

We cannot pass our guardian angel's bounds. Even when we are resigned or sullen, he will hear our sighs. - St. Augustine

and dismissed the feelings. After I returned home, I received several phone calls urging me to take the position. One of the deans, in whose presence I had felt curiously uncomfortable, was particularly persistent. After his third phone call I had a terrible nightmare in which I dreamt that he tried to choke me and nearly succeeded in doing so. I woke up shaking because I could still feel the pressure on my throat and was unable to speak. I tried to calm myself and convince myself it was just a bad dream, but the terror haunted me, and the feelings of dread which this nightmare produced refused to go away. While I felt silly being affected so severely by a dream, I decided to call my friend in California who had recommended me for the dean's position. She had accepted the presidency of the university several months earlier, and I trusted her. I confessed what I thought were unsubstantiated fears. She was silent for a few moments, then said, "Don't answer any mail or phone calls from the university. I've wanted to contact you but it isn't safe. I came across some information and decided to resign from the presidency. Don't worry if you don't hear from me; I'll be in touch later."

Later was a long time, but I eventually found out that this small, wealthy, private university was part of a large laundering operation for drug money. The U.S. government had received information that eventually led to the shutting down of the institution.

The world in which we live since the terrorists' attacks of September 11, 2001, has become a battle ground between the forces of light and dark and of good and evil. What I felt on that campus in California over a decade ago was the influence of evil, but I didn't recognize it. It took a powerful and terrifying nightmare to literally shake me out of my indomitable optimism. On a much larger scale, the attack on America has made the whole world aware of the power of insecurity in the face of evil.

In the United States we have lost our innocent belief in the safety of our own turf. The feeling of imminent danger surfaces with every security alert issued by the U.S. government. With suicide bombs and daily loss of lives around the planet, evil seems to be spreading like wildfire. But I don't believe this is the spread of evil, but rather evil becoming more obvious and more visible. The good side is that the visible is easier to fight. The dark angels have stepped into more or less perceivable positions. We are no longer fighting total unknowns. Between them and us are the angels of God. Too often we forget that the angels of God far outnumber the dark angels.

Anyone alive today is aware of the threat of violence and evil in today's world. We associate evil with darkness and fear. The good news is that the Light is more powerful than the darkness. When the electricity goes out in a dark movie theater, the darkness can be dispelled by as little as one lighted match that pierces the dark environment. Light is the more powerful force. It is the force of God. To protect ourselves from the dark

Reputation is what men and women think of us; character is what God and angels know of. - Thomas Paine

angels, all we have to do is surround ourselves in a cloud of light, the protective Light of God. With faith in the goodness of God and the presence of angels, we can feel safe.

God is Love and Light. Light of Goodness and the Evil of Darkness prevail in a world in which opposites define each other. Good is defined in contrast to evil, and evil is defined in its absence of good. So it is with light and darkness as well.

The most famous of the dark angels is of course Lucifer, also known as Satan and the Devil. Like the good angels, the bad ones are prohibited from interfering in our lives. They can enter our realm only with our permission. We give this permission in ways in which we are not aware, and that is with negative emotions of fear, doubt, anger, and hatred. By engaging in negative emotions, we call forth negative energies. Angels are messengers. Their messages are thoughts, and thoughts are energy. When we have negative thoughts, we give power to negative energy. This is the invitation which the fallen angels await.

We can escape the clutches of the evil angels whenever we choose to do so, simply by reverting back to positive thoughts. Since angels are not capable of intervening in our lives except by invitation, we can uninvite them when we realize the negativity of our thoughts. The best way to do so is to ask for the light of God and God's angels to surround and protect us. Whenever we call on our Guardian Angel, the evil angels lose the power which our negative thoughts had given them, and thus their energy is dissipated.

The dark angels can never destroy the angels of the light, the angels of God. While total darkness can be dissolved with a single light source, making a room with even one window completely dark on a sunny day is much more difficult. The Light and the Good will always triumph over Evil. Evil thoughts can be overcome by good thoughts. For example, on December 22, 2001, Richard Reid was overpowered by passengers and crew members on American Airlines Flight 63 after they saw him attempting to light the fuse to a bomb hidden in his shoe.

Psychologists tell us that three out of a hundred people are deviant from the norm. I am not aware of any statistics that tell us the percentage of truly evil people, but the chances of coming face to face with a mass murderer or a suicide bomber are relatively rare. The percentage of basically good individuals far outnumbers the percentage of the truly evil. Sadly, we don't get very many Good Samaritan stories in the media, but random acts of kindness occur every day.

Two thousand five hundred years ago, the Greek philosopher Empedocles theorized that there are two forces dominating the cosmos, the force of creation and the force of destruction which he called "Love" and "Strife." His belief was that Love will always prevail because it is creation. Strife or hate can never destroy love; it can only transform it into something else, theoretically into apathy (inactivity) or anger and hatred (strong forces). Creation cannot be destroyed because then destruction would also be destroyed and that is not possible. It can only be transformed just like the candle transforms the dark into light in a pitch-black room. Modern physicists have confirmed Empedoles' theory with the "Second Law of Thermodynamics" and the preservation of energy and matter which scientifically states that nothing can be destroyed, only transformed. This is very good news, because by this definition there is no death; we are merely "translated," as the seventeenth century poet John Donne explains, "by God."

You may have noticed the tone in my writing becoming increasingly more serious in this section on the dark angels. That's the professor in me trying to understand this battle between good and evil which is a book in itself. What teachers aren't taught is how to take themselves lightly. I'm still working on that. So let's go back to the light where the angels are, and to the fun stuff.

Angels can fly because they take themselves lightly.
– C. K. Chesterton

Messages from Angels

Angels are all around us whether we believe in them or not. We can't see them, but they are there. They watch over us, and they protect us. They inspire us to act. They guide us. They give us ideas. In fact, they are thoughts.

When I think of an angel, I think of light. I taught my children when they were young to imagine themselves surrounded by white clouds whenever they were scared, as a way to visualize the angels surrounding them and protecting them. It's natural for us to look up toward the sky when thinking of the Divine because we don't usually see God or the angels next to us. In our mind, we receive messages from God on the wings of angels, because they can fly between heaven and earth. This visual image is the reason why artists consistently depict angels with wings.

We tend to perceive a physical distance between God and our world. This "distance" between the divine and the human world is bridged with thought. Angels can carry God's messages because their purity and innocence do not distort the communication between the Divine and the human realm. They are pure energy and pure thought.

Angels are energy, and just like a lightening bolt, they seem to come from the sky instantaneously. But that's not really where they are.

When we think of angels consistently, we see them eventually. But who of us is truly consistent in our thoughts? Scientists have determined that we think approximately 65,000 thoughts a day; most of them are about conversations and events of the past twenty-four hours. If only ten percent or 6,500 of our thoughts were about angels, we would be able to communicate with them on a daily basis.

Since most of the time we don't listen, and often we don't know what to listen for, angels choose a variety of means to communicate with us. Sometimes they appear as gut reactions, sometimes as a feeling, and sometimes as an idea or an inspiration. Angels make themselves known to us as thoughts and energy. We can feel their presence. Sometimes these thoughts or energies take on visible form. Sometimes they come in the form of gut reactions, or a sudden "ah...ha" recognition or realization.

And sometimes they startle us out of our stupor in impossible ways. I had an experience several years ago that I was reluctant to share even with my loved ones because I thought they might think my already active imagination had finally taken me to the edge of reality.

One morning, I picked up the daily newspaper and read the headlines as I walked to the kitchen. I noticed an article about an artist and her "vivid dreams" as I put the paper down on the kitchen counter to fix myself a bowl of cereal. After I put the milk back into the refrigerator, I reached for the paper and suddenly saw a little golden angel earring lying right under the words "vivid dreams." It was my earring. How did it get there? A chill ran through my body as I walked briskly to my bathroom where I had taken both earrings off the night before. There was the other earring lying on the counter by itself. I was alone at home. There was no logical explanation of how that earring could have appeared on the newspaper in the kitchen. The phrase "THE IMPOSSIBLE IS POSSIBLE" kept running through my mind. I knew this was a message I could not ignore.

For some time, I had been giving angel lectures and wondered how I could make the information I have collected reach a larger number of people. Not long after the angel earring miraculously appeared on the newspaper, I received a phone call inviting me to participate in a radio interview on angels. Another author of angel books and I were featured on national public radio. Maybe that's why the angel appeared as an earring.

Sometimes angels appear in human form. Several years ago, when I was on an airplane flying home shortly after my father died, a gentleman sat next to me. I wasn't in the mood to be friendly. Filled with grief, I didn't feel like talking to anyone and lowered my head toward my lap and the opened book on angels I pretended to be reading. Undaunted, the vibrant, white-haired gentleman began a conversation which turned out to be very interesting. He managed to hold my attention and keep me from crying. As the plane arrived at the gate, he tipped his hat and said "You know I could be one of those you are reading about." The angel book was still open. I looked down and saw only print, nothing that would identify the content of this book. When I looked up, he had already gone. Quickly I grabbed my purse and followed the line of passengers, hurrying to catch up with the mysterious gentleman, but he was nowhere in sight. The thought of having sat next to an angel was awesome. I wish I had known! There are many stories of angels appearing as strangers and then disappearing without a trace. I have no doubt my friendly seatmate was an angel. His message to me, hidden in the delightful stories he told, seemed to be "Don't grieve; your father is okay."

Angels appear to us in whatever form catches our attention most effectively and reach us on different paths and by many different means, sometimes for reasons we don't understand and sometimes for very obvious reasons. The idea of a guardian angel is widely accepted and yet quite often never recognized.

He who has fed a stranger may have fed an Angel.

- *The Talmud*

Guardian Angels

It is not uncommon for angels, especially guardian angels, to appear in animal form. While it is easy to become distrustful of human behavior and manipulation, animals are more direct in their communication with us. I came across the story of a little three-year-old boy who had walked through a gate left open in the backyard. He wandered into the national forest adjacent to his home. Since his parents thought he was playing in the backyard, it was some time before they discovered he was missing. Even after the police and a search party arrived, a full day passed before they found the little boy in the forest. He was asleep, cuddled, and kept warm by a stray dog that had befriended him. In the midst of the joyous reunion and tears of relief, no one noticed the dog slipping quietly away. The boy's parents had resolved to give the stray dog a home for life, but the angelic canine was nowhere to be found.

Guardian angels are protective forces that are around us throughout our lives from birth until death. Children are more often aware of these protective angels than are adults. A young child talking to his or her imaginary playmate is more than likely speaking to an angel. Guardian angels have intervened as unseen forces in moments of danger or crises. An invisible hand that holds back a child running into a busy street or catches a falling infant is the hand of God acting through the Guardian Angel. As we grow into adulthood, society teaches us to become "realistic" and to let go of our fantasies. As a result, our angel playmates gradually move into daydreams and eventually out of our consciousness.

Bringing angels back into our conscious mind is easy to do. Doing so consistently and often is hard. I don't know about you, but my good intentions, like exercising daily, eating only healthy foods, and even flossing, just can't seem to make it past a few days when incentive is lacking. Nevertheless, reconnecting with our angels can be done. In our mind's eye, we can see and feel angels because angels are thoughts, and thoughts are energy. Thoughts produce feelings, and energy produces sensations, both visible and invisible. Sometimes the presence of angels is perceived through a warm feeling inside, sometimes simply as a presence. It is through the conscious awareness of sensations such as these, that we begin to get reacquainted with the angels.

In the past, when I realized I have not thought about my angels for a long time, I reconnected with them by inviting the angels back into my conscious mind. What we think about becomes real and what we don't think about doesn't exist for us. That is one of the reasons why thought is so powerful.

The process of angel awareness begins with the mental habit to think about the angels consciously on a regular basis, and our guardian angel in particular. An effective way to make this a part of our daily experience is to set aside a period of uninterrupted time, five or ten minutes, more if possible. Find a comfortable place where you will not be interrupted by phone calls, friends, or family members. I personally like the bathtub and always light a candle. My favorite time of day is early in the morning, but late at night is just as effective if you prefer to stay up late. It's good to drink a glass of water before settling comfortably into your private space. You can either sit quietly with your visions of angels, or you can do the angel meditation in the next chapter.

For every soul, there is a guardian watching it.
— **The Koran**

Angel Meditation

Close your eyes. Envision a favorite setting in nature, either in the mountains, by a river, in the woods, along the sea shore, or in the desert, wherever you would feel most comfortable when you are alone. In this special spot, build a gazebo, a vacation home, or a palatial residence. Envision yourself inside the completed structure, relaxing in your favorite spot. You are at ease, comfortable, and completely relaxed. Now invite your Guardian Angel to enter and introduce himself or herself. Although angels have no gender, we sometimes see them as male or female. Don't be surprised if more than one angel appears. While each soul is accompanied through life by one special Guardian Angel, there are usually many more angels around us. Ask your angel any questions you wish. You can even ask the angel's name. Converse with your angel until you are ready to leave this special place. Once you have constructed this setting in your mind, you can return to it in consciousness any time you wish. It is particularly helpful during times of stress to withdraw into your inner vision and regain a sense of balance and safety in this special place. When you return often, it will become your sanctuary, and you will begin to feel your guardian angel more consistently.

Meditation is the dissolution of thoughts in Eternal awareness or Pure consciousness without objectification, knowing without thinking, merging finitude in infinity. – Voltaire

Asking Angels For Help

When I first began asking the angels for help, it was urgent and immediate. Some time ago, I stepped on the brakes because the car in front of me came to a sudden halt. I knew I couldn't stop and screamed almost out of instinct, "Please help me, angels!!!" The road was wet and my car went into a tail spin. It ended up on the other side of the road facing the opposite direction. I sat there for a while, stunned and shaken. Like a mantra I repeated, "Thank you, God!... Thank you, Angels!... Thank you, God!...Thank you, Angels!"

Over the years there have been several traffic incidents where my plea for instant help came in the form of a scream. The most emotionally difficult and traumatic one was one day, when I picked up my young children from school. I was driving through a neighborhood adjacent to the elementary school when a four-year-old little girl darted out from her front yard into the street. I swerved to the left to avoid hitting her, screaming, "NO! NO!, God! No!!!!!!" I jumped out of my car to see her seemingly lifeless body lying on the pavement several feet in front of the bumper. Her eyes were open but didn't seem to respond. I kept screaming, "Oh God! Please don't let her die, God, please don't let her die!!!! Please send your angels. Please help us!!!" I watched her mother carry her into the emergency room. Later that afternoon I called the hospital to find out how the little girl was doing and if I could visit her. I was told she was in shock when she came to the emergency room but was released with only mild abrasions and was sent home an hour later. My immediate response was a long repetition of, "Thank you, God! Thank you, Angels!"

There are a number of ways we can ask our angels for help, and all of them involve the thought process. Angels are always ready to help us if our request is sincere, comes from the heart, and is motivated by what is good. As discussed earlier, angels attempt to get our attention in the form of feelings or gut reactions when we don't ask or we forget to ask for help. However, they cannot alter our situation unless we invite them to do so. Except in cases of immediate physical danger where our subconscious will to live calls them into action, angels cannot bring about changes without a specific request from us, because angels are not permitted to interfere in our lives without our permission.

Since angels are sent forth by God, they can act only on behalf of that which is good. But even when requesting what we may perceive to be good, it is important to remember to be careful what we ask for, because we will probably get it. It is extremely important to be conscious of the impact our request has not only on us but on those close to us.

Angels cannot, no matter how heartfelt the request, intervene in the lives of others at our request. You may want to influence the actions of another person by asking your angel to change their behavior. But even if it is in the best interest of a loved one, the request cannot be carried out by your angel. However, you can ask your angel to talk to the angel of the other person and appeal to the angel of your loved one to carry your message to that individual. For example, suppose you have a disagreement with a family member or someone you love, and the other person is so unreasonable, that he or she will not listen to your point of view, no matter how hard you try. It may even get to the point where the two of you can't speak without yelling and screaming; or worse, you can't talk to each other at all. In your heart, you really want to make peace with the other person, but you can't see any way to do so. In such a situation, you can ask your angel to communicate with the angel of your loved one. That way, your chances that he or she can be reached are much greater. By directing your thoughts to your angel who passes them on to his or her angel, you are sending your loved one additional positive energy.

In our mind, we are constantly talking, usually not to ourselves as much as to others, continuing previous conversations and coming up with clever responses that hadn't occurred to us earlier. Since the other person is probably having similar one-way mental conversations with us, neither one is heard. If we direct our conversation to our angel, and make the request that our angel convey the message to the angel of the other person, that person is more likely to get the message. That way the angel's message doesn't have to fight the interference or static of the person's own mental

Angels speak to all of us.

chatter. The angel's communication will come in the form of a realization or an idea, a warming of the heart, or some other positive feeling. This may happen over a period of time, but if the request is made consistently with love and good intentions, the positive messages will eventually be received.

One request I like to make when a situation seems incomprehensible is to ask the angels for the highest good of all concerned. Sometimes we become the recipients of a message sent from the other person's angels that help guide our behavior.

When my brother was killed in an airplane crash, my mother's grief turned to bitterness, especially toward those closest to her. It was difficult to communicate with her. Again and again, I asked my angels to speak to my mother's angels to help her see what she was doing in her anguish. It took years, but my patience was greatly rewarded when my mother's love for me once more surfaced in a most beautiful way.

The nicest thing about making requests of the angels is that there are so many angels around. They are easily identified by the role that they play. For example, if we have misplaced an important item, we can call on the Angel of Lost Items to help us find it. Similarly, we can ask the Angel of Creativity to help us with a project, or the Angel of Memory to help us remember something, the Angel of Health to guide us toward physical, emotional, mental, and spiritual well being. We can even ask the Angel of Parking Spaces to open one for us in a crowded parking lot. Nothing is too insignificant to the angels as long as the request comes from the heart.

It is important, after making a request, that we allow our faith to take over. Negative emotions such as fear, doubt, and anger, overshadow faith. Anxiety acts as a barrier, making it difficult to accept and understand the help of the angels. Fear, doubt, and anger make such strong demands on our feelings, that we do not sense the subtle messages our angels send.

It is faith that brings forth the good, faith that dissolves negativity and faith that activates an awareness of angels in our consciousness. In good faith we can make any heartfelt request of the angels and our request will, in time, be granted. That is the grace of God.

The golden moments in the stream of life rush past us, and we see nothing but sand; the angels come to visit us, and we only know them when they are gone. - George Elliot

Angels and Miracles

Just like angels, miracles aren't something we notice until they're right in front of us. And again just like angels, they are a part of our everyday life. The famous psychologist, motivational speaker, and author of such best sellers as *Erroneous Zone* and *There is a Spiritual Solution to Every Problem*, Wayne Dyer is an avid tennis player. On a number of occasions he has spoken of seeing the tennis ball stopping in mid-air in front of him. While I admire Dr. Dyer greatly, I had a little bit of a hard time imagining a tennis ball stopping just like that in mid-air. Well the angels taught me never to doubt miracles.

At breakfast one morning, I poured myself a glass of orange juice when the bottle slipped out of my hand. In mid-air it turned upright, and I was able to catch it before it could hit the counter and shattered the glass. I smiled and thanked the angels and thought of Wayne Dyer's tennis ball. I decided if he had the courage to talk about his tennis ball, then I could write about my bottle of orange juice. It really doesn't matter whether anyone believes me or not. Thanks, Wayne!

The wonderful thing about angels is that once I let them into my conscious awareness, they began making themselves known more and more frequently with little daily miracles not always as dramatic as the orange juice bottle. They truly have a sense of humor, but they also take their job as protectors very seriously.

On the way to work one morning, I was stopped at a red light. It was early, and there was not much traffic. For some angelic reason, I didn't pull into the intersection when the light turned green. Instead, I sat there for a few seconds, then moved my foot from the brake to the accelerator. At that very moment, a car came speeding from the left, going what seemed like ninety or a hundred miles an hour. Had I crossed the intersection when the light turned green, I wouldn't be writing about this miracle.

Another miracle involves my mother. For years she struggled to take care of my father who had succumb to Alzheimer's Disease. No one person should have to endure what she went through, but she refused to accept outside help, and putting my father into a nursing home was out of the question for her. Understandably, my mother became increasingly irritable and lashed out at the only one who was close to her – me. I lived five hundred miles away and dreaded the bi-monthly visits because it was so difficult to take the verbal abuse. I made little or no attempt to defend myself because I knew it was her pain speaking.

To brace myself I took a small Bible with me. Hoping the angels would guide me to a passage that would provide some strength and comfort, I opened the Bible randomly. My eyes fell on the words "behold, I have sent unto thee a present of silver and gold" (I Kings 15:19). This verse had absolutely no relevance to my situation at all, so I decided that this time the random opening of the Bible didn't work, and I went to sleep.

The next morning after breakfast, I sat down at the dining room table to grade papers. My father sat nearby with an empty gaze looking nowhere. My mother kept walking past me, back and forth, and I braced myself for another verbal onslaught.

She disappeared for a while, then returned with a big Tupperware container filled with her valuable jewelry. She pulled out a solid gold necklace and bracelet, a silver bracelet, several gold rings, and a diamond pendant, and one by one handed them to me. My mother put her Seiko watch on my wrist and told me how grateful she was that I always come to help her. I was deeply moved and speechless. I had asked the angels for strength and comfort and received it along with silver and gold! The angels had tried to tell me the night before, but of course I didn't get it.

*I saw the angel in the marble
and carved until I set him free.*

- **Michelangelo**

Angels and Sex

In an interview about her latest book, the famous sex therapist, Dr. Ruth Westheimer, stated that the Bible is the world's oldest sex manual, and that God is the ultimate sex therapist. She points out that sex is an integral part of the physical experience of being human and that it is the expression of the deepest form of love between two people.

Sex is the blending of a physical and spiritual consciousness. In its purest form, orgasm is the physical culmination of our spiritual connection to another person. It springs forth from a deep feeling of love and affection.

Dr. Ruth suggests that our society misinterpreted God's message concerning sex, and has turned sex into something to be hidden or worse, something "dirty." Instead, we should perceive sex as God's greatest gift, the highest form of love and respect for one another. When viewed as an expression of God's gift, sex can become a beautiful means of communication between two people.

As messengers, the angels have always played a role in the love life of humankind. The most famous angel in this category is, of course, the one we call Cupid. Angels delight in matchmaking, in bringing together two people whose mingled life will produce love, kindness, respect, and perhaps children.

The angels don't abandon us after the honeymoon is over and the children are running through the house. On the contrary, the angels are always there and available for our requests for help. So when the romance seems to subside, we can ask for their assistance. We cannot ask our angels to force actions on the one we love when the love seems to ebb. But we can ask our angel to address the angel of our mate to inspire him or her with the desire to show love and affection in variety of ways. As a result of our request, relayed by our angel to his or hers, our beloved may suddenly feel moved to speak more sweetly, to buy flowers or candy, or a greeting card. The angel of our mate may in turn inspire us with actions our mate finds desirable. All of this will eventually lead to the culmination of love, to the sacred sexuality.

Although it may seem strange to ask the angels to help us out with our sex life, angels are available to us for any kind of help we address. Who else would we dare to ask if we can't afford sex therapy? The Angel of Sexual Fulfillment can inspire us with ideas, or relay messages to its counterpart in our

mate. If it is a matter of re-triggering our own sexual desires, we can ask our angel to help us reach that point. We can even ask the angels' help when physical problems interfere with sexual expression.

Music is well said to be the speech of angels.
– **Thomas Carlyle**

Impotency in men and lack of sexual responsiveness in women are serious concerns that frequently originate from emotional complications. When physical reasons have been ruled out, an appeal to the Angel of Sexual Competence may prove to stimulate a miraculous recovery.

In invoking the help of the angels, we are reaching into the deepest aspects of our own inner being. Conversations with the angels are conversations with the most sacred part of ourselves. When we communicate with the angels through our thoughts, we are communicating with the Divine.

God created man in his own image, the spiritual image. Psalm 91 suggests He created the angels to help protect us in this perilous physical realm. Angels themselves have no gender; they are neither male nor female, and thus themselves take no interest in the sexual roles of human beings. Their actions are pure love, the expression of God's love to mankind.

Angels raise our spirits.

The Angel of Death

One of the most difficult things for us to deal with in life is death. More difficult than our own death is the death of a loved one. Whether it comes slowly after a lengthy illness, or suddenly, we are never prepared, and the pain is incredibly deep.

Angels are always there, ready to assist us. Though we may not consciously ask for their assistance in a moment of intense pain, it is our subconscious mind that summons these messengers of God. Since angels are not permitted to intervene in our lives, it is our instinctual life force that calls them into action in moments of imminent danger. Although they may not intercede, angels do send signals and messages of all sorts. It is good to become more conscious of instincts, gut reactions, and feelings because those are the most common ways messages from angels appear. Unfortunately, we have been taught to be skeptical and analytical and have learned to ignore these gentle nudges in our consciousness.

An angel appeared to me in a dream and showed me a scene of my brother's death. There was speed, an impact, then a fiery crash. I shot out of bed and ran to the phone to call my brother to convince myself he was still alive. When I looked at the clock, it was two-thirty in the morning. My heart was pounding. Then I told myself "it was just a dream." Imagining my brother's anger over his little sister disturbing his sleep, I took my hand off the receiver and never called.

This dream haunted me for months, but slowly ebbed into memory. My mind tried to understand something that could not be explained. I had not yet begun my spiritual journey. Seven years later, almost to the day (it was Valentine's Day) I was the one who got the phone call in the middle of the night. My parents informed me that my brother's private plane had gone down in a fiery crash. The nightmare from seven years ago had become reality.

Why did the angel deliver the death message seven years before it happened? It was years after this tragedy took place in real life that I began to understand the angel's message. The purpose of the message was NOT to foretell the future. Looking back, I now understand the angels were paving a spiritual road for me, one that would eventually draw me away from the atheistic views I held at the time.

Having the premonition of my brother's death did not make dealing with his death any easier. On the contrary. Guilt crawled into moments of grief and made me think that if only I had told him about my nightmare, maybe he wouldn't have died. Obviously, knowledge of my dream would not have prevented my brother, the pilot, from flying, nor would it have stopped the airplane from crashing into the southern California mountain.

So was it the Angel of Death that awakened me with a nightmare so many years ago? Yes, but the Angel of Death is not the grim reaper that we have been taught to fear. We tend to find death and darkness frightening because it represents the unknown. However, the Angel of Death is also the Angel of Rebirth.

Ancient Greek pottery painting c 450 B.C.E

This angel helps us make a transition from an old way of thinking to open up new perspectives to us. The reason the Angel of Death is associated with darkness and fear is because it reaches into the darkness of our consciousness to bring us light.

It was the Angel of Death that enabled me to help my father cross the bridge from a physical existence to a spiritual one. It was difficult to watch my vibrant and energetic father succumb to Alzheimer's disease. I did not receive a dream to warn me of the years of suffering before his death. But when the time came, the Angel of Death was there, not to rip my father away from his loved ones, but to guide him gently to where my brother was waiting for him. Eight years later the Angel of Death came for my mother and taught me about another side of death, a rather beautiful side.

My mother had come to live with me because she was not able to take care of herself anymore. Our relationship had long been one of opposites. I knew she loved me, but after my brother's death and especially in the difficult years of my father's illness, I often felt she didn't like me.

After losing their son, my parents understandably lost their zest. My father eventually withdrew into emotional numbness and the emptiness of Alzheimer's disease, and my mother gradually became cynical, bitter, and aggressive to family members, friends, and sometimes even to strangers. She had good days when she was wonderful, but these days seemed to be dwindling in numbers.

Death makes angels of us all.
— Jim Morrison
The Doors

Having her in my home became an enormous emotional challenge, but I was the only remaining child and the only one she could turn to.

A year and a half after she moved in with me, my mother was diagnosed with cancer. I focused all of my attention on her during that time. Her emotional and verbal attacks on me stopped, and she began telling me how grateful she is for everything I was doing for her. As the cancer progressed, she struggled with pain but kept her dignity. She always insisted on dressing herself nicely every day, even though on most days she saw no one but me. Her hair was neatly combed; she wore her jewelry and a little bit of makeup. To the very end, she never looked ill, and even the Hospice nurses commented on her healthy appearance.

One morning my mother could no longer walk on her own. After the doctor told her that nothing could be done, my mother decided she wanted to die. I reminded her of her granddaughter's wedding only three weeks away. My mother was a very proud woman. She said if she could not walk down the aisle of the church, then she didn't want to go to the wedding, even in a wheelchair.

Two days later, the Hospice nurse who came to check on her, told me my mother had only a few hours left. To me, Hospice nurses are angels! Had she not prepared me, my mother might have died by herself. That had been her greatest fear. My greatest fear had been walking into her room and finding her lifeless body. Instead, I was able to call my older daughter, Erika, who came over with her fiancé, Dan. My younger daughter, Monika, lives two thousand miles away. I called her at work. Monika immediately left work and rushed to her apartment so she could be with us on the speaker phone. I offered to call her back so the long distance charges would go on my phone bill, but she insisted that with over five hours left on her phone card, she had enough talk time.

My mother had been in a coma for several hours. I held one of her hands, and Erika held the other. Because my mother had said she wanted no tears, my daughters started telling funny stories involving their grandmother. All four of us were laughing. Suddenly, I felt a gentle squeeze from my mother's hand. A few seconds later Erika felt a squeeze from the other hand.

The Hospice nurse stopped by briefly. Seeing us all together and hearing Monika's voice over the speaker phone, she commented on how much love she felt in the room and left again.

I felt comforting angels around me, but didn't see them. The sun was shining through the bedroom window, and the conversations went on and on. Dan observed that my mother must really like the farewell party. Over the speaker phone I heard a giggle of agreement followed by, "I bet she'll use up all five hours for her party!"

Exactly five hours from the time the phone rang, my mother took her last breath with a smile on her face. Her soul gently slipped away, surrounded by love. The angels stayed with us; we felt no grief but rather peace and comfort. I'm sure the smile on my mother's face was seeing the Angel of Death who must have been kind and gentle.

On the day she told me she wanted to die, my mother thanked me for making her death so beautiful. At the time I didn't know what she meant. Now I see it as her last special gift to our family. My mother and the Angel of Death taught me that death really can be beautiful when love is all around.

I had asked my mother weeks earlier to send me a sign after her passing that she was okay. My mother thought it was a strange request and shrugged. After her death, I dreamed that I stood next to her dead body on the gurney. Suddenly she sat up and said, "Why are you so sad? I'm not dead!" After having the same dream three times in the week after her passing, I had no doubt that my mother was doing well and living on in the spiritual realm.

A few weeks later, a rose bloomed in my front yard in the dead of winter. My mother knows I love roses.

The angels do not acknowledge death as we do. For the angels it is an opportunity to guide the soul into the spirit realm. There is no end, only a new beginning. If we allow it into our conscious mind, the Angel of Death helps make that transition easier for us as well as for the dying. And if we are receptive to the help of the angels, then we can begin to understand that the Angel of Death is also the Angel of Spiritual Rebirth who reaches into the darkness to bring us to the light.

Silently one by one, in the infinite meadows of heaven
Blossomed the lovely stars, the forget-me-nots, of
angels. - Henry Wadsworth Longfellow

Be an Angel

You've probably heard the phrase, "be an angel," or "you're an angel!" Maybe you even used a similar phrase yourself. Is it possible, then, for us to be angels? Well, the answer is yes and no. We can't really BE angels – they have no gender and they are pure spirit – but just like the angels can take on human form, we can play the role of an angel. Or we may allow an angel to use us for angelic reasons.

As messengers, angels are thought and energy. Energy can move so rapidly that it is invisible. Or so slowly that we can see and touch it. The angels of God appear in all forms. As thoughts, ideas, or feelings, they are, of course, invisible. Sometimes, when we become receivers of messages, we temporarily become angels.

An angel came to the rescue one day, when my daughters were visiting their father. Nine-year-old Monika and her stepsister were playing in the school yard of the elementary school some distance from the house. They decided to race home on their bicycles and got separated. With her stepsister out of sight, Monika was suddenly lost. She walked down the railroad tracks remembering that the tracks run near the house. What she didn't know is that she walked in the wrong direction. Monika walked and walked for what seemed like hours. Nothing looked familiar. With only the family dog trotting obediently next to her she was getting more and more frightened. Then she saw a clearing with some construction vehicles and men standing around. It made no sense because the men were not working on anything. Panicked and alone, Monika began to cry. With tears streaming down her face, she ran up to one of the men, a rugged, red-haired, and red-bearded man. She said she was lost and didn't know how to get home. The man told her to get into the truck, that he would take her home. Worried about her dog, she asked if he could come along too, and what about the bicycle? With the bicycle, the dog, and little Monika in the truck, the kindly man crossed the open field and headed straight for her father's house. A few minutes later she was safely back home. She ran to her room, without saying a word to anyone.

It was a long time before my daughter told me about this incident, because she was afraid she would get in trouble for accepting a ride with a stranger. When Monika finally did tell me the story, I paled and reminded her of the bad things that can happen to little girls who get into a car with someone they don't know. She responded by saying, "You always told me to listen to my feelings. I was really scared when I didn't know where I was. I kept asking God and the angels to help me find my way home. When that man told me he would take me home, I wasn't scared anymore. The funny thing is, *I never told him where I lived*. He just pulled up the truck in front of the house and then disappeared. "I think he was an angel, Mom!" At that point, I couldn't argue with my daughter. I know she was right. While I would never advocate a child getting into a car with a stranger, I do believe an angel saved my daughter that day.

God sends his angels in all forms. Sometimes when we do kind things, we become messengers ourselves. In that limited sense, then we can all be angels at various times in our lives. The full-time angels are the ones that vanish without a trace when we turn to look for them.

"We can do anything we want to do if we stick to it long enough."

-Helen Keller-

Angels, Time, and Money

Time and money, like angels, tend to vanish in thin air. We experience time "flying" and money "talking." Similarly, angels appear and may speak, but then are gone in a heartbeat. All three, angels, time, and money, are concepts. We don't see the concept, only the symbols which represent them. We seem to understand them only in the form of the meanings we attribute to them.

I've never "seen" time fly, but I've certainly felt it. And I have felt money "talking" but my ears didn't hear it. All three play a more important role in our lives than we are often aware. They impact us emotionally and physically and affect our mind and our body. And we never seem to get enough of any of them.

We "see" angels not as physical beings, but as images in flowing robes with wings. Sometimes they appear as light, disappearing the moment we blink. Like angels, money and time are elusive. Every once in a while I think I have enough money to pay for something only to find out I don't. Or I think I have enough time to get to an appointment and discover I am running late.

Time flies when we're having fun. Time is valuable to us. We may waste it, but we don't want anyone else to waste our time. We are very conscious of time. In fact, we are so conscious of it that we watch it all the time, which is why we wear watches! Time, like angels and money, is relative to our specific experiences. When we are having a good time, there never seems to be enough of it, but when we are bored, it seems endless. Time doesn't exist without us. Hours, minutes, and seconds are human inventions. Two thousand five hundred years ago, Pythagoras, the Greek mathematician, divided the day into twenty-four segments which we call hours. Over a thousand years later, when the mechanical clock was invented, the hour was divided into sixty minutes. With the development of watches in the twentieth century, we added the second, and computers, known for their impatience, have added the nano-second.

Now that we've reduced time to such tiny increments, we seem to be losing time or at least running out of time, all the time. It seems like we never have enough time. And if time is money, it only makes sense that we're constantly running out of time AND money.

While we tend to be careful not to waste money, it often seems to fly more quickly than time or angels. Sometimes we spend most of it even before we get the next paycheck. Like time, money doesn't exist without us. It only has the symbolic significance we give it. The same amount of paper and ink are used for a one-dollar bill as are used for a hundred-dollar bill.

Despite the value of the paper on which money is printed, it remains the same regardless of the number of zeroes. However, the value attributed to that paper can be the difference between a hamburger and a week's worth of groceries. Money receives its legitimacy from the value we attribute to it. Likewise, this applies to time and angels. Neither time, nor money, nor angels can affect our lives unless we give them permission to do so.

The determining factor of the role played by angels, time, and money in our lives is our attitude toward them. If we fear that we have no guardian angel, our wall of fear blocks the conscious mind from becoming aware of heavenly beings. Since fear creates reality, if we fear poverty, we will experience poverty; if we expect wealth, we will attract wealth. This is true of time as well. Thus we create a self-fulfilling prophecy.

I used to rush around the house and complain of never having enough time. One day, my father said, "If you say that often enough, it will be true for you." Many years passed before I realized the wisdom of my father's words.

We empower angels, time, and money with our faith. Through faith, we create a positive mindset and affirm the dignity of angels, time, and money in our lives.

In the United States, we honor the system of money by imprinting our currency with the phrase, "IN GOD WE TRUST." As a medium of exchange, money has a spiritual essence. If we did not all agree to this concept, our system of money wouldn't work. With money we are honoring one another as well as our spiritual source. Similarly, we have agreed, universally, to adhere to the twenty-four-hour system of time. Like the consensus on the value of time and money, the existence of angels is validated by faith. A spiritual attitude leads to the certainty that we will always have enough time, money, and angels.

Those who practice the spiritual approach, find that the more we give, the more we receive. The more we love, the more we are loved. The more we respect others, the more we are respected. The more we trust, the more we are trusted. This is also true of angels and time. The more time we give, the more time we seem to have. The more time we spend contemplating angels, the more we sense them around us. When we trust the angels to help, they do.

If we try to control the angels, they slip away from us, just like time and money. With faith and an open our heart, we become more sensitive to the presence of the angels. Our thoughts become our reality. Faith makes us whole.

So can we ask the angels for more time and money? Of course! Will they deliver? Believe it or not, they will! So why don't we get it? Mostly because we think we don't deserve it. It's our thoughts that prevent us from receiving what we ask for.

Buddha with Angels
India, c. 150 B.C.E.

All that we are is the result of what we have thought. If a man speaks or acts with an evil thought, pain follows him. If a man speaks or acts with a pure thought, happiness follows him, like a shadow that never leaves him. – Buddha

Angel Thoughts

If angels, time, and money are pure thoughts that we perceive as symbols, how can we be more receptive to what we want? How can we turn our dreams into reality? The answer is communication.

Learning to communicate with angels and the Divine is easier than communicating with ourselves. The saying "We are our own worst enemy" contains more than a grain of truth. When searching for solutions to our problems, we tend to examine our actions, our feelings, our environment, and of course anyone involved in the problem. We seem to be reluctant to face our own thoughts.

Thoughts produce feelings which in turn spur action, and action brings reaction from others. When confronting a problem, we tend to focus on our emotions rather than on our thoughts. Therefore, we tend to ignore our thoughts.

Have you ever watched your thoughts? I tried it when I wanted to purge myself of negative thinking in order to make contact with my angels easier. In the morning I programmed my mind to watch what I was thinking and count the number of negative or judgmental thoughts I had. I couldn't keep count, because there were a lot of them at first. I began practicing dismissing negative thoughts and replaced them immediately with positive ones. It took a long time for this purge to work, yet I still find myself thinking unproductive and self-defeating thoughts. But I am learning how to remove negative thoughts from my mind.

Given the duality of our universe, it is often necessary to acknowledge unpleasant truths and acts of evil. Equally important is to remember the constant power of light, the good, the angels, and God. I am pleased to say that thoughts of angels occupy more and more of my daily 65,000 thoughts.

Thanks to angelic inspiration, I began to realize how much our thinking affects not only our emotional state but also our physical well being. Even everyday language reflects this with such statements as "that just turns my stomach" or "that's a pain in the neck." With such words and thoughts, we empower these ideas in the same way we empower money, time, and angels. It manifests through our thoughts and the power we attribute to the idea behind them. Consequently, if we repeat it often enough, we may end up with a stiff neck or an upset stomach. Unless we have taught ourselves to pay attention to our thoughts or the words we use, we don't make the connection between our spiritual and physical sides.

Angels try to communicate with us, but often fear, doubt, and insecurity create a barrier that not even our conscious mind can penetrate. The barrier is the product of our insecurities: fear of failure, fear of success, fear of inadequacy, fear of not being worthy, doubting our ability to cope with what we ask for, doubting our own power to reason, doubting the angels and their power, hiding our fears, our perceived shame, our deepest feelings . . .

The way to overcome such hidden enemies consists of opening our heart to God and to the angels, by paying close attention to our thoughts and to the feelings they generate. We gain self-esteem and the power to defeat our various fears by respecting ourselves and the integrity of our decisions, our choices, our authenticity. In this way, we become powerful spiritual beings and draw the angels and all good things to us. It takes practice, but we can all do it if we want to.

Giving thanks for the good things in our life helps us realize how much there is to be grateful for and makes it easier to think positive thoughts. The more positive we become, the more likely we are to sense the presence of our angels. Playing with the angels lightens our load, for they can teach us to fly!

Angels manifest themselves in us as thoughts and energy which are inspired by God. We are the reflection of the Spirit of God, and His kingdom dwells within us. God is Love, Light, and Spirit, and we are an individual soul of Love, Light, and Spirit, the

ALL. Just as we would not worship ourselves or our thoughts, we don't worship the angels because they are part of us. We do, however, worship that of which we are a part, the All, the Love, the Light, the Spirit, GOD.

In my end is my beginning.

– T. S. Eliot

Elisabeth Stein, Ph.D.

The author is a professor at Tallahassee Community College in Tallahassee, Florida, where she teaches Humanities, Philosophy, and World Literature. She has over thirty years of teaching experience, and has conducted numerous seminars and workshops on a variety of topics including, Interpersonal Communication, Public Speaking, and Angels. With her lectures, Dr. Stein has touched the lives of numerous participants, many of whom return for additional classes, seminars, and workshops. A glimpse of her passion can be found in *Angels - The Divine Connection*, where she reveals her personal experiences with the angelic realm. She shares her perceptions in the hopes that others will find the comfort and peace our angles transmit to us.

For information on lectures and workshops contact
Educational Seminars and Training
P.O. Box 4363
Tallahassee, FL 32315-4363
Angels-TheDivineConnection.com
850.386.5978